DATE DUE

Demco, Inc. 38-293

NOV 0 1 2010

The Eternal City

PRINCETON SERIES OF CONTEMPORARY POETS

Paul Muldoon, *series editor*

KATHLEEN GRABER

The Eternal City

POEMS

PRINCETON UNIVERSITY PRESS

Princeton & Oxford

Copyright 2010 © by Princeton University Press
Published by Princeton University Press, 41 William Street,
Princeton, New Jersey 08540
In the United Kingdom: Princeton University Press, 6 Oxford Street,
Woodstock, Oxfordshire OX20 1TW
press.princeton.edu

LIBRARY OF CONGRESS CATALOGING-IN-PUBLICATION DATA
Graber, Kathleen.
The eternal city : poems / Kathleen Graber.
p.   cm. — (Princeton series of contemporary poets)
ISBN 978-0-691-14609-6 (cloth : alk. paper) — ISBN 978-0-691-14610-2
(pbk. : alk. paper)
I. Title.
PS3607.R323E74   2010
811'.6—dc22   2009049321

British Library Cataloging-in-Publication Data is available

This book has been composed in Adobe Garamond and Aldus

Printed on acid-free paper. ∞

Printed in the United States of America

10   9   8   7   6   5   4   3   2   1

Now let us, by a flight of imagination, suppose that Rome is not a human habitation but a psychical entity with a similarly long and copious past—an entity, that is to say, in which nothing that has once come into existence will have passed away and all the earlier phases of development continue to exist alongside the latest one. . . . Where the Coliseum now stands we could at the same time admire Nero's vanished Golden House. On the Piazza of the Pantheon we should find not only the Pantheon of today, as it was bequeathed to us by Hadrian, but, on the same site, the original edifice erected by Agrippa; indeed, the same piece of ground would be supporting the church of Santa Maria sopra Minerva and the ancient temple over which it was built.

—SIGMUND FREUD

Contents

III

The Eternal City

Tolle! Lege!

Here's the spring
And with it transmogrified
Yataro becomes Issabo.

—Issa

In truth, I have less faith in the gods than I do in the chair
I passed one night set out with the trash on John Street,
even though it seemed to me then to be already beyond saving
& I was too tired to try to lift it & carry it away.
Stripped of its cushions & fabric, the frame, by moonlight,
looked like some primitive technology, a fragment
of the heavy plough scientists dug from a Danish bog
& dated through pollen analysis to the 4th century B.C.—
the wooden wheels they knew it had had having long since
turned into peat. What I know of conversion
I learned while cleaning the sticky shelves of the icebox,
a glass sheet exploding as one end hit the sink's hot suds.
For a single moment, as fissures crackled along the body,
I held something both whole & wholly shattered,
then, form gave way, it broke a second time, & was gone.

William James loved best those changes that burst upon us.
He hardly cared that they rarely stuck or that Augustine
in the garden had been preparing all of his life to be seized.
Hearing the children chanting, *pick up & read, pick up*

& read, the Saint's eyes fell upon the Epistle to the Romans,
written by Paul, the one who, having seen the Savior
revealed on the road to Damascus, left even his name behind.

Outside, men are clearing the lawns, blowing the last
of winter's leaves into copper hills before shoveling them
into the bed of a truck. They've been at it all morning,
laboring a long time to unswaddle one acre of earth.
They pass the window & everything churns, as if the room
has been swept up in a blizzard of wings. When, decades ago,
in a dilapidated tenement slated for demolition, I caught
my own reflection in a heavy mirror affixed to a wall,
I smashed it & packed my pockets with as much of myself
as I could. Later, I poured the bits into an old milk bottle
& gave my idol a battered doorknob for a head. Augustine
believed he could almost glimpse that greater kingdom
wavering before him. *Aenigma*, he writes, suggesting the face
in the mirror, though his mirrors would have been bronze
& someone somewhere would have spent all of his days
pounding the world into something that small & shiny
& thin. And still, it is not easy to make out what is sought.
Someone somewhere is, even now, delicately turning
the maple spindles of a chair at a lathe. The landscapers
drive off & all the little houses resettle—
the way plovers in the dunes, having stood to stretch
their throats into the diffuse light of spring, ease down again
into the reeds. And so it is with the disquieted self, which,
startled almost at the start from itself, seems always now
to be awaiting its own return. The soul, Augustine reminds us,
loving itself, loves what is lost. He recalls the shepherd
who upon finding the missing lamb raises it up
& strides home happy. Mile after mile, he rejoices
beneath his burden of flesh. He bears the warm belly
across his glad shoulders. The pink mouth bleats at his ear.

I

The Magic Kingdom

And as in the daily casualties of life every man is, as it were,
threatened with numberless deaths, so long as it remains
uncertain which of them is his fate, I would ask whether it is
not better to suffer one and die, than to live in fear of all?

—St. Augustine, *City of God*

This morning, I found on a slip of paper tucked into a book
a list of questions I'd written down years ago to ask the doctor.
What if it has spread? Is it possible I'm crazy? I've just returned
from Florida, from visiting my mother's last sister, who is eighty
& doing fine. At the airport, my flight grounded by a storm,
I bought a magazine, which fell open to a photograph
of three roseate spoonbills tossing down their elegant shadows
on a chartreuse field of fertilizer production waste.
Two little girls emptied their Ziplocs of Pepperidge Farm Goldfish
onto the carpet & picked them up, one by one, with great delicacy,
before popping them into their mouths. Their mother, outside
smoking, kept an eye on them through the glass. After my cousin died,
my father died & then my brother. Next, my father's older brother
& his wife. And, finally, after my mother died, I expected
to die myself. And because this happened very quickly
& because these were, really, almost all the people I knew,
I spent each day smashing dishes with one of my uncle's hammers
& gluing them back together in new ways. It was strange work,
& dangerous, even though I tried to protect myself—

wearing a quilted bathrobe & goggles & leather work gloves
& opening all the windows, even in snow, against the vapors
of the industrial adhesives. Most days now I get up late
& brew coffee, & the smell rises from the old enamel pot
I've had to balance under the dark drip ever since the carafe
that came with the machine shattered in the dishwasher last month.

One morning I found a lump in my breast, & my vision narrowed
to a small dot, & I began to sweat. My legs & arms felt weak,
& my heart thrashed behind its bars. We were not written
to be safe. In the old tales, the woodcutter's daughter's path
takes her, each time, through the dark forest. There are new words
for all of this: a shot of panic becomes the rustle of glucocorticoid
signaling the sympathetic nervous system into a response
regulated by the sensitivity of the hypothalamic-pituitary-adrenal axis.
And as I go along, these freshly minted charms clatter together
in the tender doeskin of the throat as though the larynx
were nothing if not a sack of amulets tied with a cord & worn
around the neck. But I tell you I sat on the bathroom floor for hours,
trembling. And I can tell you this because the lump was just a lump,
& some days now I don't even dread the end although I know
it will arrive. The garage is filled with buckets of broken china.
The girls chased each other & waved their arms casting spells,
the trim of their matching gingham dresses the electric pink
of the birds' wings. They turned each other into princesses
& super-girls & then, they pretended to change back.
Oh, no. You forgot to say forever! they took turns repeating
with dramatic dismay, melting into puddles of themselves,
their sandals & sunburned knees vanishing beneath their hems.

Dead Man

Some are born to sweet delight.
Some are born to endless night.

—William Blake, "Auguries of Innocence"

We spend our lives trying to grasp the premise. William Blake is not, for instance,
William Blake, but rather a 19th century accountant from Cleveland on the
lam for murder & the theft of a horse. In the closing scene,

he is going to die, & so is Nobody, his half-Blackfoot, half-Blood guide.
Sure, this is a Western, a morality tale
                              about a destiny made manifest
through the voice of a gun & a hero whose mythic flight from innocence

destroys him. But we all come to the end of the line soon enough.
The obvious just seems wiser
                              when Nobody says it. *Time*, it turns out,
is the most common noun in the English language, as if by constant invocation,

we could keep it at bay.
                              Yesterday, I sat in another state on a large rubber ball
in my brother's basement bouncing my newborn nephew in my arms.
His mother, on the phone with a friend, asks what we should fear more,

the hobo spider or the poison that kills it. I want to whisper into his ear
something that feels like knowledge:
                              Once upon a time, there was nothing

& one day, there will be nothing again. This is the faraway place

to which his tiny weight calls me. If he could understand the words, I think,
he would know what I mean, having only just sprung himself
                                                            from that fine sea.
Sometimes we coo to soothe him: *Don't cry, Little Bird. I know, I know.*

But only the roar of the vacuum finally calms him,
                                                    for nothing sounds as much
like the lost world of the womb as the motors of our machines.
The root of *travel* means *torture,* having passed from Medieval Latin

into Old French. As the action opens, Johnny Depp, shot in black & white,
is already rocking into night on a train. And soon, he will begin his dying.
This is not to say that the inky band fanning across the morning blue

of a kestrel's tail feathers
                            has no meaning, or the first fingers of rust
coming into bloom on the green enameled chassis of a Corona typewriter
left in the rain.
                Direct observation, the naturalist Niko Tinbergen assures us,

is the only real thing. Perhaps this is what I should tell him.
                                                    Or that this moment,
too, is a part of some migration. Every snow bunting composes its own song,
& a careful watcher can tell one kittiwake from its neighbor by the little dots

on the tips of its wings.
                        The most used verb is also the most humble—
merely *to be.*
                Nobody can teach to William Blake the auguries of William Blake.
We are, instead, our own vatic visions, bumbling prophets. Our sense of ourselves

as invented as film.

    Later, in an ocean-going canoe lined with cedar boughs,
he will drift out into cold breakers, two bullets in his chest. But, here,
in his small hat & wire glasses, he still seems

          sweetly comic. He holds up a letter;

someone's promised him a job. His fancy plaid suit makes him look like a clown.

Florum Principi

Prince of Flowers, who set out to give an order to the multitudes, my collection
is so different from your own,

                            which you filled with the carefully pressed

lectotypes of bear's ear & foxglove & carpeted with the pink *Borealis*
which blooms so briefly midsummer beneath the Lapland pines.

Mine holds two tarred boxes & boatless oars & the broken sonar equipment,
which came with the house & goes on sleeping on a shelf in the garage,

despite the revving of a neighbor's Jet Ski—on a hitch in his driveway,
spewing exhaust one moment & stalling the next—

& the honk of a car alarm that sounds all afternoon without reason.

Who can say how the world made strange by our understanding of it
would seem to you, who went to ground before Darwin asked

whether *a beneficent and omnipotent God would have designedly created
parasitic wasps*, or Charles Willson Peale exhumed the hull of a mastodon

in a thunderstorm in Newburgh, New York, to prove beyond question
that a mighty species might cease to be. Among specimens of butterflies

you christened *agamemnon* & *mnemosyne* & the skin & bones
of the John Dory *Zeus faber*, a fish whose flank is said to bear the stain

of St. Peter's thumb, what could have seemed more improbable than change?

The turf roof of your cottage in Hammarby still puts forth houseleek
& the narrow-leaved hawk's beard. And the shoots sprung from the seeds

of the empress's honey-sweet *Corydalis nobilis* still threaten to overtake
the yard.
       Here, however, the Surfside Diner is now an information center

& the Three Coins Motel & the Ebb Tide have been razed to make way
for vinyl-clad condominiums no one has the money to build.

Their sandy lots, still littered with a few bricks, accumulate beer cans
& the twisted frames of aluminum beach chairs. Dandelion & cocklebur.

Aster & thistle.
       And if I'm feeling blue, it's because I've been looking
all morning at the old photos I've promised to send to my brother,

who has a new son & can, therefore, stare into the untended past
& not be bent.
       My senior year of high school, I drank too much

& rode my bicycle around until dawn, then sat at the counter of the beach grill
eating bacon & eggs for free because the waitress was my best friend,

who ended up strung out & disappeared after falling in with a junkie
named Joe who worked in the kitchen. When my grades slipped,

no one phoned my house or suggested Guidance get involved.
My troubles were less than most.
       I can't account for what the people

in the pictures might have been thinking, why they didn't demand
their daughter be home at night in bed. In this one, my mother is smiling.

She's had her hair done; she's wearing those big gold hoop earrings
I've got in the drawer.
                        Because you knew two words were enough

to separate chickweed from mallow, I want to talk to you about the soul
& the question of when we become irrefutably ourselves, a question

theologians have debated for centuries, going so far as to ask at what point
miscarried fetuses must necessarily be human & ought, so being, to be

blessed.
          Were I not Alexander, the great Macedonian conqueror proclaimed
at Corinth, *then I would be Diogenes*.
                                        I cannot tell you exactly why

this story charms.
                  At eight weeks, a careful observer can see all the parts:
the tiny specks of the eyes, ten discrete toes,
                                              but the chromosomes—

which not even the pre-Socratic Democritus, who hypothesized
the existence of the uncuttable atom, could have imagined—

are there from the start.
                        Yesterday I read about a genetic disorder:
the afflicted are driven to hurt themselves & those they love. It is,

by all evidence, extremely rare—a single, inexplicable glitch in three billion
bits of code. Case studies include men who thrust their hands into their mouths

& bite off their own fingers. Some bite off their lips.

They beg to be restrained.

There will always be those who insist everything is getting better,
even when we can't discern it.

But this must really have been what you felt

in your grove of plums or in spring under the Siberian crab apple,
whose blossoming limbs appeared from a distance to be burdened

with snow.

Today is the first day of autumn though it's only August.

It's the first day though—the air & the light pregnant with something

like despair or the sudden stillness along the coast when the tourists
have gone.

We don't want to be lonely, but we are. *Disappointment?*

More like the promise of a disappointment we're disappointed hasn't come.
Melancholia, Hippocrates might have suggested, & it's a beautiful

appellation—

a constitution under siege, he thought, to too much black bile.

Three o'clock. A yellow wind whispers its one note over & over

into the willow's ten thousand salt-blistered ears.

Just now, only this—

something so small not even you have given it a name.

The Drunkenness of Noah

after Jean-Louis Chrétien

Most afternoons Margaret Boone's father threw his crumpled Pabst cans
into their cold fireplace, took off all of his clothes, & passed out
in the living room's recliner. And when my mother became too ill
to bathe herself, she sat on a plastic stool in the tub
as I worked my way around her with a sponge. No one is shocked:
nearly none of it is too painful or too foul. Routine, even,
after a time, for all the kids in the neighborhood, to simply spread
her father's fallen shirt across his lap. And how common
to dream, like Tristan Bernard, that our parents are still with us:
to dream them being so cruel that we wake almost happy
to find them gone. *How very fortunate*, he writes.

In Bellini's oil painting of Noah, drunk & sleeping, the good sons—
having already tucked the edge of their rosy cloth from hip
to hip—continue to avert their eyes while Ham mocks from above
his luminous father's frail exposure. And so the story goes
that for his shameless gaze Ham was cursed & the sons of Ham
became the slaves of slaves to the children of their father's brothers.

When I was twelve, I returned from school to find my mother
had been taken to the hospital. I wondered why no one had come
to get me out of class. Soon, though, it was clear: it wasn't
the kind of hospital people die in; it was, instead, the kind of place
someone very tired goes to rest. Just now, I stopped everything,
going to the closet & putting on this worn red wool undershirt,

even though it is summer & when I opened the door
& pushed the hangers to one side I had actually been looking
for something else. Perhaps this is as close as we ever come
to stumbling into understanding if understanding is the familiar
weight of a heavy sleeve against the arm inside it & madness
is its opposite, a soul caught out in the open not wearing
anything at all. My father brought me only once to visit her
there & no one spoke of it later, whatever it was that had passed.
The truth is I often laugh when I don't know what else to do.
The room was blue & very small & she seemed small & blue
inside it. Sometimes we find a way to say what cannot be said.

And sometimes we never speak that for which we could
only too easily find the sounds. Noah lived 350 years
beyond the flood & became a man of the earth, intoxicated
in old age on the vines he'd raised. Even in our silence,
we are told, we carry the Word. This morning in the shower,
I looked down & saw my mother's bare body asleep in mine.
Noah's nakedness fills the canvas, making it impossible
not to look. As though simply to recall the tale is a sin
whose penance is to live knowing you have somehow
made it happen again. The memory flickers, almost
without detail, shorter than a dream, & threatens to go out—
illuminated not by an orange flame but by a brutal whiteness.
The snowy blast from a television screen. Or a fluorescent light
with a faulty ballast which hums & winks all night in an empty hall.

Fitzcarraldo

The camera rests again on Klaus Kinski's face: changeable sky, a tangled jungle
we cannot crack.
                      Franz Joseph Gall—the phrenologist whose undertaking

has become as absurd to us now as the dream of carrying a steamboat
over a red mountain of clay—knew, at least, that the brain is the opera house

of the mind. He called Individuality *the memory of things* & sat it so low
on the brow, the first frontal convolution, that the singular self seems to conduct us

from the bridge of the nose.
                              It is both possible & impossible to alter the world
with a gramophone. Fitzcarraldo on the roof of the wheelhouse answers back

the drums with the imperfectly captured voice of Caruso.
                                          And again today,
my dog races to the porch responding, her canine profession of faith,

answering back in kind to the *Über-dog:* the town's noontime alarm.
Language was the first faculty to be located; a head injury to the *Island of Reil*

might leave a patient speechless. And Carl Wernicke gave the name *anomia*
to the disease of having lost all of one's nouns: with no sound for *aria*

or *apple*, all desires contract to the categorical, to merely wanting *something to eat*.

Rainy matins. *Prayer*, I say, for *woofing* & for *fetch*. I stride out,

despite the drizzle, toss the ball to the far end of the yard, but the dog won't play. She shakes her head, flapping her ears, waits by the door to be let back in.

Yet from across the harbor, the hammers of day laborers framing new houses continue to pound. Perhaps there were words once for every hunger:

a list for the dark, unique lonelinesses inside each throat, each dome

of folded hands.

The memory of melody must become for the deaf composer the music itself.

And isn't one phrase just as good as the next?

We get the idea: a child

points to a cow & says *Ellie*, the name of the black & white terrier who lives

next door.

As though we could trade *rubato* for whole note; rubber plant for *Hevea brasiliensis*. *Colonist* for *pilgrim*. Rubber plant for *weeping tree*.

The Third Day

And God said, Let the earth bring forth grass, the herb
yielding seed, and the fruit tree yielding fruit after his
kind, whose seed is in itself, upon the earth: and it was
so. And the earth brought forth grass, and herb yielding
seed after his kind, and the tree yielding fruit, whose seed
was in itself, after his kind: and God saw that it was good.
And the evening and the morning were the third day.

—Genesis 1:11–13

This morning I locked myself out again, realizing just
as the door of the complex's communal laundry clicked shut
behind me that my keys were still atop the triple loader.
I'd been thinking about the senator I'd seen last night on television
& the language—*terroristic, Islamo-fascist enemies of freedom*—
he'd used to describe those whose ideologies conflict so starkly
with his own. And Augustine's question: is evil a thing in itself,
or merely, as he came to argue in the end, the absence of good.
Later, when I finally find a neighbor—glad she's home,
glad she is willing to lend me her keys so I can retrieve mine—
we stand a few minutes chatting. She's from Minnesota
& dislikes the winters here. Her eyes rest on a plastic toboggan
& the bicycle beside it, training wheels rusting in three inches
of mud. It's February & we've had rain all week. The temperature
is already above fifty & although the limb-whips of the willow

are bare, its trunk is splotched & spongy with pale green moss.
I can see that the kids who like to roughhouse after school
have shattered someone's terra cotta planters & a small holly—
its roots dressed now in only their own black ball of dirt,
its carnelian beads aglitter—has been tossed out onto the walk.

Augustine was haunted by his gang's adolescent theft of pears,
a transgression nearly without motive: the pears were so hard
& so ugly, inedible, in fact, that he knew, even as he took them,
that there were better ones at home. It's difficult to say
what he means by *unmaking*, but this is what sin is & does,
he warns, as we stray, *disordered,* away from the perfection
which made us toward the *nothing* from which we are made.

By late afternoon, the sky brightens & they are all at it again,
using slingshots made from forked twigs & rubber bands
to pelt one another with the sharp pods of the sycamores.
What would we do without our fellows? Adam,
the Saint argues, took the apple even though he knew
the serpent had deceived her, for he could not bear imagining
Eve lost in the wilderness alone. A small child is beating a tree
with a baseball bat trying to knock more ammunition loose,
& the prickly spheres, which horticulturalists call *fruit,*
dance & dangle—like the thurible the Monsignor swung
sometimes at mass. I sat in the pew beside my grandmother.
The words being spoken were Latin. I studied the bright cloaks
in the windows & the scuffs on my shiny black shoes.
Across the open field, a beagle, caught up too tightly
in the rope which has been used to tether him to a porch,
starts to howl & the squirrels scatter. And an old nest, dull
& high up—still holding only a few fists of air—begins to quake.

The Heresies

That the truth is both visible & blinding. That the alloyed belly of the world—
nickel & iron—poured from the great madness of Wisdom, who,

expelled from the Divine Light for seeking the cause of what is cause-less,
wants now only to be rejoined with what she has lost. That the sea

& the rain & especially these few beads of condensation, collecting here
on the half-lit pane—out of nowhere—are her tears. The cold stream

from the faucet is an elemental being wholly unlike ourselves. The wheat
weeps at the harvest & the loaf, some say, cries out as it is torn. That we

must be the voice for all things locked in silence. That the good suffer
in order that the less good may be spared. On the evening news, mortars

are falling. And in Jenkintown, a man is trying to achieve *ethical ecstasy*,
having given all of his money to charity, donated a kidney to a woman

he's never met. If he could sacrifice a liver, both eyes, his one good heart,
he tells the reporter, he would. In a book of Renaissance woodblocks,

Vanity clutches a hand mirror; Industry tends the hive. And Justice
dangles from her left hand a delicate scale while, with her right,

she brandishes a sword. On the last page, there are the Sirens, forever busy
tuning their harps. The song is disaster. But it's their role to seem

to be what they're not. It has been written that the wisest should guide us,
& Zell Kravinsky, one kidney remaining, argues his odd but logical case.

His life isn't worth more than the life of anyone else. He's got enough
parts to keep five or six people alive. Tonight, instead of a sensible

& sympathetic cosmos, only the self peering out of the pot's still water,
the plate, the polished ladle. Doubter, boil the potatoes. Sit down to eat.

Because we cannot leave, yet do. Hitch the ass & the horse
to the cart. That grace might save us. That all matter is brought forth

in ignorance & grief. Every blessing is molten. Sew the cotton to the wool.
That our lessons may instruct us. That the life of reason will bring us to joy.

Un Chien Andalou

The only philosophy which can be responsibly practiced in the face of despair is the attempt to contemplate all things as they would present themselves from the standpoint of redemption.

—Theodor Adorno

I ride the train, after not having ridden the train in a long while. Outside, another deserted warehouse district.

                        The woman beside me leans back,
rests an opened Catholic missal on her lap. On the left page, Jesus, in full color,

holds up the cup of wine.
                       Early spring & the cloudbank that scattered
delicate flurries all morning is disbanding now to the south.

Just after dawn, I watched as two nurses lifted my arm above my head

& using a long latex bandage forced the blood down & out of the limb
before inflating the double cuffs of a tourniquet below my shoulder.
And when the surgeon slit into my elbow,
                       I felt it all, despite the anesthesia.

Yet, it was never more than a person could stand.
                       In the 19th century—

we've seen the black saws displayed in glass cases—whole legs
were removed routinely, with little more than some whiskey & a stick

between the patient's teeth.
                              And on the news, after a bomb blast, a man
explains. *It is like this: you look down and find a child's hand at your feet.*

My swollen fist, hours later, aches in its clean cotton sling, sweating off

something mineral—the smell of rocks in rain—like the birth-bruised head
of a thumb-sucking infant, tucked down in the cradle & refusing
to be roused from its dream.
                              I had forgotten how much I love the engine,

the procession of cars swaying behind, the way believers,
wrapped in brown robes, trail a plaster-of-Paris crucified Christ
down Grove Street in Jersey City.
                              In another minute, the rails will pull us under

the bedrock of the river & deliver us to the basement of the station,
inevitable & waiting, on the opposite shore, like the end of any good tale.

As even those of us without faith pray to be plunged, somehow, into mystery,

for fear we will otherwise be forsaken by what is unfathomable inside.
My country is at war in a country at war with itself.
                              We presume
& we do not presume
                    to understand. A voice calls my name: *The doctor*

will see you now. And then, on the platform, the loudspeaker reports
The 10:37 local is operating on time.
                              Which is to say, that hand,

the stubborn hand of a child in the street, will not become

the hand of a child, but remains, instead,

                              a black & white film with subtitles
that arrives in a red sleeve from Netflix,
                            the one by Buñuel & Dalí
about García Lorca. The one we've given another name: the one we call

surreal.
        As, now, I look into broken eyes of a factory—its windows smashed
all around—& see clear through. Its brick depth filled, for an instant,
with April sky.
            And when the woman turns the page, there is Mary Magdalene

in the garden, discovering the stone rolled away. In the tomb,
not darkness, but angels & their light—that cold, impossible blue.

The Synthetic A Priori

What objects may be in themselves, and apart from all
this receptivity of our sensibility, remains completely
unknown to us. We know nothing but our mode of
perceiving them. . . . With this alone have we
any concern.

—Immanuel Kant, *Critique of Pure Reason*

At a church rummage sale, I study the perfection of shadows
in a painting by Caravaggio, although what I hold
is only a small print of Christ—its frame broken—dining
at Emmaus with three of the Apostles. And because the table
is dramatically, if not unbelievably, lit, the bowls & pitcher
& loaves send their dark crescents onto the immaculate
white cloth. When the Savior raises his hand to offer a blessing,
its shade deepens further his crimson smock. *Tenebrosus*:
that rich, convincing darkness. As though the master understood
that the obscured world only seems to us somehow
even more familiar, as though our sense of our own unknowing
had at last been made visible—even if what we do not know
cannot itself be seen. The future's drape, the carnival fortunetellers
of my childhood might have called it, but also the now's,
displayed as it is—so many unmatched cups & saucers, old coats
& wicker baskets—all around us. At a party last week,
someone said *verisimilitude*. We were huddled on a tiny porch.
It was the first cool night & the wine had no conclusion.

The talk turned quickly to shepherds & the pastoral & then,
to opera, before someone recalled a horror film he'd watched
late one night with his brother. In black & white vignettes,
an evil tree stump possessed by the spirit of an executed prince
hunts the scheming tribal elders who have destroyed him.
A former pro wrestler in a costume of wire & rubber bark
& wearing a permanent scowl lumbers after vengeance
in the confusion & fear of 1957 on a half-dozen root-legs,
driving his victims into quicksand or toppling himself over
upon them. Though here the point is the teller's small brother
& the boy's allegiance, even in a state of *suspended disbelief*,
to what we call *sense*. How, he wanted to know, suddenly
unusually earnest, did the tree manage to get itself up again?

Yesterday I spoke to a friend who is despairing: back home,
waiting tables, he's dating a woman whose marriage has only
just come to an end. When he wakes, he discovers he does not
recognize himself. One afternoon, walking home from school,
I hit my best friend in the face with a book. It may well be
that she hit me. Thin pages flew out into the street. More punches
were thrown & I came away bruised. In that book, a novel
by Emily Brontë, the land is violent & unjust & we are violent
& unjust upon it. Even worse, our greatest passions
change nothing at all. Before one of us hit the other,
there must have been a cause, but I can't recall it, which makes it
seem nonlinear now, &, thus, apocryphal, both impossible
& impossibly real. I failed, though I tried, to offer comfort.

It's not that our lives don't resemble our lives. I've been alone
so often lately I sometimes catch myself watching myself—
breathing in the fresh spears of rosemary or admiring the shallots,
peeling their translucent wrappers away, centering one on the board,
making the first careful cut, lifting the purple halves.

Before stories, we were too busy for stories, too busy
hunting & suffering to invent the tales of our own
resurrections. Caught out in the kitchen's brightness last night,
the handle of the skillet cast its simple, perfected form
across the stove—pierced, like the eye of the needle, so that
it can be hung from a hook, as pans, presumably, have always been.

Outside the wind picked up. Thunder. The dog trotted off,
hid her head beneath the chair. But today: a charity sale
at Trinity Chapel & sun on the tar of the buckled walks.
In the cracks, beads of water spin into light. Tell yourself
it's simple: this is where it's been heading all along. Tell yourself
something you have no faith in has already begun to occur.

II

The Eternal City

The attic fan rattles in its hammered tin house—as seemingly ceaseless
as the body's unquiet engine. Today something's gone awry: the drone,
usually poised, a nearly silent arpeggio, has become a disinterested scream.
This is the third heat wave of July. Again the fire department
sounds the citywide alarm & then police cars wail. Rome is burning!
But Rome is not burning. Instead I am reading, in a shrill hum,
about Marcus Aurelius—because this is what I do on days too hot
to move—the heads of the red geraniums steaming in their planters—
too hot to imagine that we might send up our lives in flames.
The mind is more than a simple container, the junk drawer
beside the stove. My thoughts clang like pennies in the dryer.
O, my racket—ice against the blender's wall of glass. The Eternal City,
Brodsky writes, is like *a gigantic old brain*, one that's grown
a little weary of the world. And what have we here? Tarnished keys.
A chipped teardrop from some dining room's chandelier. The trick
must be to love both the blade & the air it shatters. A flock of birds
meets the airplane's roaring turbines. We pass the stuff from which
we're made—look, a single pocked marble & a spent emery board—
through our own propellers. The phone rings, but I don't answer
though I've been expecting it. It stops, then rings again. Still—
I don't pick up. Loneliness, our one defendable empire. Aurelius, too,
loved metaphors: *the inland lake on the island Aenaria; in that lake,*
there is another island, it, too, inhabited. O, my acrobats, in the dark
capital of nested boxes, be with me always, secure & tumbling.

Book One

From my grandfather Verus, I learned good morals and the
government of my temper. From the reputation and
remembrance of my father, modesty and a manly character.

—Marcus Aurelius

From my mother's sister Peg, I failed to learn frugality
though she would add last night's peas to the morning's eggs.
She wore her neighbors' spotted hand-me-downs
until the exhausted seams gave out & even then, she saved
the buttons. And, now, here they are. Do you know the pleasure
of the button box, a red cookie tin with a poinsettia & holly sprig
pictured on its lid? Or its smell? Rust, yes, but also another
putrefaction, the outgas of cellulose decaying. White shirt buttons
evaporating into chalk, like those effervescent tablets used to clean
false teeth. And the salt of those fingers—or have I invented this?—
which polished each disc against the sewn-to-fit mouths
of wool coats & cotton blouses. Bitter smell of the plastic cowboys
which fell one afternoon out of my brother's toy box & into mine.
And what did I learn from my brother? To love cowboys
& Classics Illustrated comic books. And, finally, to love
only the stories & set pictures aside. Here, right here,
is that same dusty metal bin, that same crumbling stack
of colorful pages—though Annie Oakley & Buffalo Bill disappeared
with the christening cups & the baby shoes when the old house
was sold. Can you see that all of this is only so much evidence now
of our never-letting-go? Half the buttons still trail old threads
from their brass shanks & a few stubbornly clutch their cloth.
But from the great orator Fronto, we learn that the best simile
must be human: Orpheus rued his turning to look back;
had he looked & walked straight ahead he would not have rued.
Truly, I tell you, I don't know how it has come again to this.

Book Two

How quickly all things disappear,
in the universe the bodies themselves,
but in time the remembrance of them. . . .

—Marcus Aurelius

Truly, I tell you, I don't know how it has come again to this.
Aurelius wanted the simple plank bed & skin of the philosopher,
but he was asked to hold an empire. He died beside the Danube
at war again against the Germans. The friend of a friend has declared
a year without purchase. Food, yes, soap & shampoo, stamps,
but no new shoes, no wine, no underwear. If she's given a gift, she must,
in order to keep it, relinquish something else. It's an arbitrary rule,
but you know—don't you?—even the most cautious can't stop.
At the bottom of yet another box of tangled black velvet ribbon,
curtain hooks, playing cards & half-full wooden spools
of Paragon silk thread, a Susan B. Anthony one-dollar coin.
It's rarely so simple: unambiguous currency, the clean tolling of worth.
I can toss out spare change more easily than this steel clamp—
the wrong size for whatever job it was meant to do. I declare this
the season of coming to order. Yet my objects defy me. What
is the value of three skeleton keys? Or this cardboard ruler that arrived
decades ago in a package of Kraft Caramels? Today I am in love again
with the Wonder Book of nickel sewing needles, a white airplane
in an oval of blue sky on the cover. I cannot tell the inherited
from the found, the legacy from what I have bred from it.
Remember the Parthians & the Quadi. Never allow them into your life.

BOOK THREE

They know not how many things are signified by the words
stealing, sowing, buying, keeping quiet, seeing what ought
to be done; for this is not effected by the eyes, but by another
kind of vision.

—Marcus Aurelius

Remember the Quadi & the Parthians. Never allow them
into your life. Last night at work, before I knew it—while I was busy
selling a tee shirt, the one with the glow-in-the-dark skeleton
in the electric chair, to Canadian tourists—an addict convinced me
to keep an eye on his six-year-old son. Slurring something
as simple as *Don't let him go nowhere*, he turned & stepped
into the congress of night-strollers on the boardwalk.
Where did he go? the child wondered. After ten minutes, he asked,
How long has he been gone? Soon, though, the father returned,
stood in the doorway of the shop, called his son's name once,
& they vanished. In his relief, the boy forgot the jarred goldfish
he'd won by tossing a coin into its bowl. At midnight, I placed it
into the opened hand of a sunburnt girl wearing thick black glasses,
knee-high socks, & a 14 gauge, surgical steel lip ring—having lost
somewhere in the past the urge to take so grave a responsibility
upon myself. The fish will die, maybe it's dead already. And I'm tired
of feeling sad. What is this other kind of vision that recognizes already
the end in sight, that foresees only disaster? Today I'm giving away
two bags of clothing I've never worn & then I'm going to run in place
at the gym while I listen to *Moby Dick* on tape. We discussed
puppets & how much he likes the big blocks at school.
We considered how slowly time seems to pass when you're waiting.

BOOK FOUR

If souls continue to exist, how does the air contain them from
eternity?—But how does the earth contain the bodies of those
who have been buried from time so remote?

—Marcus Aurelius

How slowly time seems to pass when we're waiting.
When we return from a walk, my dog begins immediately
to wait for the next. If you are waiting, Reader, I can tell you only
that somewhere it is still summer. That there are a dozen books
in Aurelius's *Meditations*, written in his old age, in his tents
on foreign battlefields as he waited through the last decade
of his life to die. Do you know Jack Gilbert's poem about a man
carrying a box in his arms? He balances his burden, shifts it,
so he will never need to set it down. My cellar is full of boxes.
In this one: bleached shells—conch, scallops, snails—
which I carried home, one by one, in a childhood I've abandoned.
The girl I was shakes her head like a disappointed ghost.
Didn't she know the sea would always bring in more? Mollusks
& the brittle, translucent husks of razor clams like the long fingernails
that grow in the grave. A box of bones awaiting a new purpose
that will not come. Archimedes gave numbers to the spiral
of the sailor's coiled rope, but the nautilus waited centuries
for Descartes to decode its elegant equiangular whorls.
Without shells, the cycloid arc, Christopher Wren concluded,
the spire would not be possible. The dog stares at the door & sighs.
We carry our waiting & our calcium carbonate cage.
We wait for the future to divine for us the past. I think of Aurelius
who thought of Epictetus: *Thou art a little soul bearing about a corpse.*

Book Five

A prayer of the Athenians: Rain, rain, O, dear Zeus, down
on the ploughed fields of the Athenians and on the plains.
—In truth we ought not to pray at all, or we ought to pray
in this simple and noble fashion.

—Marcus Aurelius

Thou art a little soul bearing about a corpse. By this we are reminded
that we are born into our dying. And this is what the priest said,
too, on Monday at the funeral of a 24-year-old girl. And, of course,
we know only by baptism—for who hasn't been inside a church?—
are we born into the Resurrection. May our sister slumber
in the earth's embroidered robe. May she wake at the feet of the Lord.
Men died each day, Aurelius, because you worshipped Rome, died
so that she might be rendered what is hers. We come, you thought,
from elements & back into elements we will dissolve. Because nothing
can arise from nothing, nothing can be lost. Our lives are so short,
you argue, can it really matter how soon they end? Fronto tells you
in a letter of a strange inscription: *Priest, don the fell.* Holy Man,
put on the pelt of your victim. What is stranger than sacrifice?
What is more heavenly than flesh? I hold a faded postcard:
Fra Filippo Lippi's *Madonna, Child and Two Adoring Angels*,
Uffizi, Florence, 1455. Some say the beautiful virgin is Lucrezia Buti,
the young nun who bore, out of wedlock, the wayward monk a son.
Often in paintings, the infant looks helpless, but, here, he has already
the face of an old man. A neighbor is celebrating a birthday.
The murmur of song crosses the open window & then, the patter
of applause. O, Rain, rain: that I may live so long as to discover what
perhaps only a Caesar can know: that all of this has been for nothing.

Book Six

Return to thy sober senses and call thyself back; and when
thou hast roused thyself from sleep and hast perceived that
they were only dreams which troubled thee, now in thy
waking hours look at these (the things about thee) as
thou didst look at those (the dreams).

—Marcus Aurelius

O, Rain, rain: that I may live so long as to discover what, perhaps,
only a Caesar can know: that all of this has been for nothing.
My brother, who is in love with Freud, tells me that our dreams
have only one actor. Whatever the costume, we each play
all the parts. Sometimes I dream I am boarding a train.
When I find a seat, I see I've left my suitcase on the platform.
When I go to retrieve it, the train pulls away. Aurelius was in love
with Wisdom, but she married him off to Duty instead.
And though he never mentions progress, his obligations
go on & on. Each morning I fill the washer, mop the floor.
The dirt returns. Have you never wished for stillness?
Not the stasis of a stoic denying desire, but a high-ceilinged room
in which nothing occurs. In the mailbox is a catalog for linens:
an iron bed with a patchwork cover the colors of lilacs; flange,
the unpleated green of new leaves. Onto a floor of rough planks,
a neat bundle of burgundy chrysanthemums has slid. Open book
on the chair's oxblood cushion. Wall like the buttery meat
of a pear. But no one is home. My lot is only this small house,
a narrow side yard. No wonder every object feels important: parched
bayberry, a few roses miraculously in bloom. Aurelius looks north
from Rome to a low wall in Britain—with what, a satellite eye?—
& how quiet even the great quilt of Europe must seem. Last night,
I dreamt I was saying good-bye to someone I love. The gray figure
resembles no one I know. Idling buses crowd the street.
I wave & turn away. That I feel nothing fills me with joy.

Book Seven

All things are implicated with one another, and the bond
is holy; and there is hardly anything unconnected with
any other thing.

—Marcus Aurelius

That I feel nothing fills me with joy. On the front page,
the charred porch of a rooming house that went up last night
in flames. And though I almost died decades ago in such a blaze,
today that past seems like someone else's. I'm hanging tintypes:
formal children, mothers with babies in their laps, couples
staring grimly ahead. I love them for themselves, for the thin metal
of their still-knocking-around. Better yet, for there being no one here
whose name I'm supposed to know. What is a photograph?
A box, a moment we can never reopen, another eulogy
to smoke & dust? When Ishmael signs on the *Pequod*,
Peleg bids him look out over the bow, for there is only water.
What you can see of the world from a far-going ship, you can see
from the harbor. And what a man can discover of life in forty years,
Aurelius writes, is the same as he would discover in ten thousand.
My family is stowed in drawers. I lift the lid of my desk—
my mother's vanity— & find two pictures: the one,
her mother's wedding in 1923, a corner torn away & the other,
her brother holding my brother, still in diapers, in his muscled arms.
When your rooms are burning, what do you save? What morning
isn't implicated in every other? I am bound by knowing
that my mother chose these; her hands set these in place.
Fronto insists that without smoke & dust there could be no altar,
no hearth. And what can be holy which fails to wound?
Our sacrament: to chase what has vanished &, finally, to vanish
ourselves. Aurelius, opening another day: *Nature will soon change*
all things which thou seest . . . in order that the world may be ever new.

BOOK EIGHT

Remember that as it is a shame to be surprised if the fig tree
produces figs, so it is to be surprised if the world produces such
and such things of which it is productive: for the physician and
the helmsman it is a shame to be surprised, if a man has a fever,
or if the wind is unfavorable.

—Marcus Aurelius

In order that the world may be ever new, my brother & his wife
are going to have a baby. Earlier this month they heard
the tiny heart: out of the whirl of the mother's organs, suddenly,
a galloping, celerity, hooves. And yesterday, they saw their child
somersaulting in the unlit paddock of the womb. It turns
its animal face to the camera it cannot possibly imagine,
raises its arm as if to wave. Gibbon traces the beginning
of the end to Aurelius's brutal son. Aurelius, who turned his back
on the blood of the Coliseum, has sired the Secutor, who straps tight
his helmet & buckler to kill naked, unarmed men before the crowd.
The rarest creatures are released into the amphitheater—
the speedy ostrich, the panther, & one giraffe, *the most gentle
of the large quadrupeds*—for him to slay. Today my friend,
just in the door from teaching *Lear* to college freshmen, phones
from across the country: he, too, is going to be a dad. He's known
for months but was afraid to say. What if something had gone wrong?
These sons are noble sons & their sons will be as well. It is a shame
to be surprised if it has been, after all, a good thing to have been born.
We bow our heads, not for fear of what they will become,
but for fear of fever, the crescent-pointed arrow of simply being flesh,
the tender arena within which there is already nothing they can do.

For Levi and Cyrus, Francis and Matt

BOOK NINE

One man prays: How shall I be able to lie with this woman?
Do thou pray thus: How shall I not desire to lie with her?
Another prays thus: How shall I be released from this?
Another prays: How shall I not desire to be released?

—Marcus Aurelius

When we are lost in our longings, Aurelius, already it is too late:
there is already nothing we can do. I have rarely desired an end
to my desires. We are so in love with our wanting. Last week,
though doctors were quick to repair it, a baby in India was born
grasping her own beating heart in her fist. Today, a Dumpster
arrives from Dave's Trash Removal & I begin to fill it. I toss in
a transistor radio that hasn't worked in years. A man walking past
asks if he can take it. Later, he returns & carries off a broken TV.
A neighbor salvages the dented gray fuse box; a girl wants a window,
a paper bag full of tangled cords. All night I listen to the wind
& the echoes of feet kicking through rubbish, like a mouse nesting
inside a drum. My older brother is dead a decade. Yet here
in its enormous gold frame is the familiar, pastel portrait
someone named Maxwell drew for our mother, an inaccurate
rendering of the two of us when we were small. I can't look at it;
I can't throw it away. *Every change is a death*, you tell yourself,
turn thy thoughts now to thy life as a child. . . . One day, I tell myself,
I will shut all the doors, leave everything behind. The museum
is showing a hundred tricked-out Victorian photographs
of that other world: the hoax of floating fairies, women haunted
by ghostly blurs. Another century & still we want to believe
in what we know cannot be true. Your words, Aurelius, have found me,
but you could not. If we are disappointed, we have only ourselves
to blame: *Wipe out thy imagination.* We fill our hands when they are
empty. We empty ourselves when we have held too much too long.

Book Ten

. . . rememberest that what does the work of a fig tree is a fig tree,
and that what does the work of a dog is a dog, and that what
does the work of a bee is a bee, and that what does the work
of a man is man.

—Marcus Aurelius

We fill our hands when we are empty. We empty ourselves
when we have held too much too long. Only once have I looked
at a lover & thought, *I am his.* Though who can say what it might be
to own our own desires? *Remember,* Aurelius writes, *what pulls*
the strings is hidden within. The old roof was replaced years ago,
but today, deadheading roses, I find another dark shard of slate
in among the roots. Only a dying man, I realize, would give away
his tools, for as soon as we finish hanging this door or sinking
these posts, we believe we will begin again building something new.
Or else we learn to bury those longings we lack the instruments
to chart. Archeologists in Mare aux Songes, Mauritius, discover
under rows of sugarcane a mass grave of dodo birds, hundreds
of bones from which to assemble, for the first time, a single complete
frame. I will never use my uncle's Stanley protractor, model No. 125,
though I took it when he asked me to. On a shelf in the bookcase,
its tiny level announces that the house has sunk. His initials—
etched with a sharpened nail one cold morning into this blue metal,
which is pitted now & beginning to rust—proclaim *dominion*
as though he thought possession could last as long as steel.
At the coronation, the shorn crowns of kings & queens are rubbed
with oil. Here, Melville insists, must be proof of the dignity
of the harpoon. I could scribe a perfect angle, seven concentric circles,
an arc. I have grown so patient. I desire less. Yet in a dream,
I catch myself, a cartographer, imperial, excavating
the old enchantment—*I am his.* Below this life, the other,
the all-but-gone: fossil & flint, the sweet field I could not own.

Book Eleven

The Pythagoreans bid us in the morning look to the heavens
that we may be reminded of those bodies which continually
do the same things and in the same manner perform their
work, and also be reminded of their purity and nudity.
For there is no veil over a star.

—Marcus Aurelius

Sweet field I cannot own: I stumble from the reeds into the wet bed
of the canal's brown muck. When the Starlight Ballroom burnt
a second time, tourists in folding chairs sat in the sand & cheered.
The pier was burning. My brother carried me on his back
up the fire escape of the Gilmore Hotel so that we could watch
from the roof, as though it were a celebration. The roller coaster
folded its thousand spindly knees. The carousel pitched its freight
of painted horses into the sea. I go & return, go & return,
like the tide's dereliction. With each pass more is missing,
amusements & men. The stars, having cloaked themselves
in the glare of day, are not the same each night. Somewhere—
even if we can't discern it—another has been born, another vanished.
Aurelius, the universe is less stable than you imagined.
What did you think it meant to turn from matter into light?
As a child, I thought that I could undo this—that I would one day
bring everything back. Time began as a black singularity,
but now only the moon's small gravity stirs the sea. Fourteen billion
years ago: a blip, then bang. I lie down in salt hay. The vast engine
of the planet, as though it were eternal, churns against my back.

Book Twelve

Where is the hardship then, if no tyrant nor yet an unjust
judge sends thee away from the state, but nature who
brought thee into it? The same as if a praetor who has
employed an actor dismisses him from the stage.—"But
I have not finished the five acts, but only three of them."
—Thou sayest well, but in life the three acts are the
whole drama. . . .

—Marcus Aurelius

What churns against our backs? The past, yes—but only
what we dream of it, asleep as we are, inside its tongueless bell.
A manic troupe of shadow-players, the wind-pitched shirt-sleeves
on the line, toss their shapes against the house, twist & untwist
around each other. Yellow jackets turn in the clover & goldenrod.
In an old book on wasps, the writer recalls a blue & white paper nest
spun beside a battlefield—imagine the tiled walls of Alhambra—
reconstituted from the tissue casings of spent shells. Tucked up
beneath my neighbor's porch, a vespa & this more common hive—
just as fine—soft, dull gray of the willow's bark. I've stuffed
every drawer & closet. In the hall for months—while I wait
for someone to come along & fix the stove—is a rubber bucket.
Inside, my mother's pie plates, a loaf pan, baking sheets, the dented
cupcake tray. If they were to disappear while I looked away,
I wouldn't know they'd gone. The Spanish King fills the shrines
of El Escorial with 7,000 relics: the cap of Sebastian's knee,
a nail from the True Cross, 132 heads of martyrs, a single thorn.
You can tame a young wasp in spring & keep it in a shoebox.
It needs only one dew-filled leaf & a little sugar to survive.

One afternoon, my mother opened her eyes & said plainly,
I guess it's time to say good-bye. But I fumble with the script;
I cannot speak my lines. So much of what I hold still stings me.
Aurelius, we never know which act we're in. We shiver in our beds.
Late in the drama, I touch, as if it were holy, whatever remains.
I have failed to learn frugality from a tin of salvaged buttons,
but learned instead *collection*: horn toggles, bright Bakelite
domes. Nearly countless, the years' cast of soiled buttons,
as though each had been snipped from the cuff of a saint.

III

Another Poem about Trains

I

Ah, Weary Traveler, in a nation of small travelers,
if you are riding just now on a train—not somewhere in Europe,
not to or from Prague or Venice, not across a great divide,
but simply disappearing, as you have always done, back into nowhere,
leaving, say, Philadelphia or Baltimore, New York,
to arrive at another New Lebanon, another Lindenwold—

& feel, suddenly, the urge for stillness, or a sense of yourself
held down against the earth by nothing but the sky,
& the idea comes to you to push back the heavy door & leap down,
not violently but gently, as wide leaves still spin each autumn—
for let us allow ourselves the solace of imagining so familiar a grace—

from the maples into the black night air. . . .

May it help you to remember that somewhere
someone is lecturing a room of students on the Ancients,
speaking of Hesiod, *The Theogeny*, speaking, perhaps,
of the great myth of Prometheus, whose very name—
& the class is being instructed just now to write this down—
means Forethought. . . .

But you are not there.

And may it help you to remember
that you will not ever be required in this life to be there again
& that you will never be so young or so mistaken
about everything as each one of them is today.

Perhaps you boarded late & the only seat left was the one
beside the door, the hard one, loaded with heavy springs
& designed to fold away. An uncomfortable spot, it's true,
straight-backed & oddly public, as though to travel at all,
you must not only love discomfort but love admitting this love—

I am thinking of you now because I'm heading back myself
into another place I'll never unpack into.
My left hip, which hasn't hurt for days, has started again
to thrum. And later, rather than catch the shuttle bus,
which will surely be waiting, I'll choose to walk a mile *home*.

Perhaps you, too, have fallen, briefly, out of love again

with the rocking rhythm,
the way—if we were to give agency to infants—
the newborn might find itself expelled forever
from the only Eden it will ever know
for having been seized, just once in the womb,
by the desire to set its small feet in the dirt. . . .

And if behind me a man is speaking into his cell phone,
attempting, with astonishing ambition, to explain to a friend
or a cousin, who has never seen the film,
the story of *Reservoir Dogs*, then I would like to say here
what must already be clear: that there can be no end
to roads & tracks in our singing, that the asphalt & rail,

more than everything we know, are the knowing itself,
which is inescapably within us. That the plot is footfall
& click-clack unfolding, as it always must, one steely step
at a time. And that Prometheus's brother, of whom
almost nothing is sung, was named Hindsight,
the one who had not the gift of predicting the story

but the gift of making sense of the story once the story was done.

II

And *If, in a hundred years, our language still exists. . . .*

Kundera speaks from the book in my lap.
He is quoting a sentence begun in a letter
fifty years ago. The language is Czech & there are minutes
enough now, for minutes, too, are the gifts of trains, to think
of the Angel of History, who—wings unfurled & painted
with a look of stunned confusion—is being blown backwards

by the force of progress itself. Ruin upon ruin
piles up around him, but he cannot turn his head to see the cause.

Early on, I couldn't stop reading meaning into things
whereas lately it seems no meaning resides.
The world, I thought, was conspiring to deliver in glyphs
its untranslatable secret. And, as for the heroic tales,
those tragedies . . . when men offered up the stories of other men's pain,
I thought what they meant was *only you can understand me.*

This strange suffering is somehow an allegory for my own.

May we forgive ourselves our innocence & our desires,
who were instructed from the beginning to look closely,
to consider how even the smallest moment might count.

One night, my father fell in love with Meryl Streep.
It happened—he recounted it often—instantly
& irreversibly when she discovered Robert De Niro
standing on her stoop. It was, he said, all in her voice.
She spoke his name, or the name of his character
in the film, just once. *Michael.*
She said it softly, but that was, he claimed, all that it took.

And years later, an actor will say that every actor
who has ever worked with Meryl Streep has fallen
in love with her. And it may well be De Niro who says it,
but he will be talking then about a different movie,
the one about two people who meet by chance on a train,

as we are meeting, or not meeting, now,
for that is only my own face reflected in the glass
& there is only this empty glare, so stale & dry, beside us both.

Meanwhile, a great city is fading in the east,

& because I am facing the wrong way, I can see it go.
The thousand blue sparks of the refineries & the uncut darkness
of the hollowed mills break finally into nothing, which is to say
into suburbs, or, sometimes, even into fields,

where in the morning—as the first green log, given over
to the first fire by a lesser god who should have known better,
must have hissed with sap—the white honeysuckle
beyond the open bedroom windows will bloom again with bees.

What I Meant to Say

In three weeks I will be gone. Already my suitcase stands
overloaded at the door. I've packed, unpacked, & repacked it,
making it tell me again & again what it couldn't hold.
Some days it's easy to see the significant insignificance
of everything, but today I wept all morning over the swollen,
optimistic heart of my mother's favorite newscaster,
which suddenly blew itself to stillness. I have tried for weeks
to predict the weather on the other side of the world: I don't want
to be wet or overheated. I've taken out *The Complete Shakespeare*
to make room for a slicker. And I've changed my mind
& put it back. Soon no one will know what I mean when I speak.
Last month, after graduation, a student stopped me just outside
the University gates despite a downpour. He wanted to tell me
that he loved best James Schuyler's poem for Auden.
So much to remember, he recited in the rain, as the shops
began to close their doors around us. *I thought he would live
a long time. He did not.* Then, a car loaded with his friends
pulled up honking & he hopped in. There was no chance to linger
& talk. Today I slipped into the bag between two shoes that book
which begins with a father digging—even though my father
was no farmer & planted ever only one myrtle late in his life
& sat in the yard all that summer watching it grow as he died,
a green tank of oxygen suspirating behind him. If the suitcase
were any larger, no one could lift it. I'm going away for a long time,
but it may not be forever. There are tragedies I haven't read.
Kyle, bundle up. You're right. It's hard to say simply what is true.

For Kyle Booten

Some Great Desire

Little Wren
Have you some great desire to ask
of the plum tree?

—Issa

Because *here* is not *here* anymore, meaning what was once
at Königsplatz has been moved to Grosser Stern,
it's no surprise if some part of it is missing. I'd hoped
to see the marble bishop holding a tiny church in his palm.
And St. Catherine with her wheel & St. Barbara
with her tower, but they are not around. Soon enough
I'll learn that I've been looking in the wrong place,
but no matter, for whatever figures from the *Siegesallee*
remained after the bombings were carted off,
buried & exhumed, reburied & forgotten long ago.

At the *Siegessäule*, I start to climb the 285 spiral steps,
which promise to deliver us to the feet of what looks—
it's true—from the streets below more like a gilded angel
than a goddess of war. But circling the corkscrew's twirls,
my legs go wobbly & I step aside to let a gang of boys pass
before I turn & head back down. The walls above the railing
are inked with red & black graffiti. A whitewashed room
beside the entrance houses models of other monuments;
above them, a placard asks: *To Whom Does the State Belong?*

Tonight a lost dog races back & forth below my window.
And a man on the balcony next door sends up a singing
that sounds like prayer. Even though the ticket seller
spoke no English, I could not not ask for what was missing.
She pointed to a diagram of the frieze that runs around
the base: bronze Prussian soldiers, who have their own tale.
When I shook my head, she shook hers & gestured
again toward stairs, which lead to the portico & its fresco,
worked out in burgundy & blue & gold glass tiles,
of Germania reborn. Even if we had had a vocabulary,
I'd still have had a hard time explaining what it was
I wanted—a set of long-lost marbles, which now seems odd,
even to me. Warm twilight, thunder, a little rain, then more.
In the apartment directly above, a baby begins to cry.

The mother walks from end to end, end to end. Shushing.
But the infant goes on crying, refuses to be consoled.

Three Poems for Walter Benjamin

LOGGIA

> In the years since I was a child, the loggias have changed less than
> other places. This is not the only reason they stay with me. It is
> much more on account of the solace that lies in their uninhabita-
> bility for one who himself no longer has a proper abode.
>
> —Walter Benjamin

It must, in winter, be, for a midday hour or two, a nearly windless well
of light. But in late July, another asylum: an almost chilly green-gray
shade. If a side door hadn't been left open, I'd have never known

this one was there.
                    Here, then, is the reason the swings & slides
in the sunny corner parks are deserted. And here, Benjamin says,
is the tiny grove where the city-god itself safe-keeps space & time—

they ripen like the neighborhood toddlers, fall in love. Even now,
one thunders on its plump legs after the other.
                                    This morning, still only
a half-step from dream—as a little girl skips rope on the cobbles

& counts, *acht, neun, zehn*—I remember that I am in Berlin, a place
where I don't know anyone at all. And when she begins to sing, the song
sounds surprisingly familiar, yet I cannot place it. I cannot make it mean.

Unheimlich.

      Uncanny. Freud spends pages sifting the etymology
of the word. But like a street hiding so many secret gardens, its semantics
suggest nothing is itself all the way through.

                       At the Gemäldegalerie,

I stand before *The Adoration of the Shepherds*, considering the sky
beyond the humble scene. Eerie glow of a solar eclipse, but this
is that other wonder, even more unlikely, darkness diluted by a star.

As a child I liked to climb the jack pine behind our house & shimmy out
along a limb onto the roof of the old garage where no one could find me.
I don't remember now why I wanted so badly to be alone.

                            Adrift

in the unrecognizable moment, who doesn't try to work backwards,
looking for the bend around which everything turned? If the caryatides
had somehow slipped their burdens to stand beside his cradle,

Benjamin knew their lullaby had contained too little of what would come.

Today I said almost nothing & just once: *I'm sorry.*

                          No Deutsch.
In the world & not.

           In 1888, a British neurologist detailed epileptic seizures

during which the sufferers never lost awareness. Rather the everyday
was suddenly shot through with something else: color, music, a strong sense
of déjà vu.

      Not a yard, but a courtyard: linden & bicycles. Dumpsters.

Hydrangeas. Heavy pink roses nodding beside a fly-curtained compost bin.

And yesterday, on Lessingstrasse—
Had I lost my way in a dangerous spot
trying to find the Tiergarten?—there in the papery weeds, a plaque

with blue letters: *Nelly Sachs. Kinderheit.*

Hughlings Jackson writes *a doubling of consciousness* & *diplopia*
to describe the haunting hallucinations his patients felt.
And Freud
makes his strange case about strangeness after lifting a single line

from a nearly forgotten novel nine volumes long: *What we call Unheimlich,*
one character tells another, *you call Heimlich.*
Dear ghosts,
I'm sorry. Who can understand? What we call History you call *home.*

The Telephone

And just as the medium obeys the voice that takes possession of
him from beyond the grave, I submitted to the first proposal that
came my way through the telephone.

—Walter Benjamin

The handmade copper phone of Austria's last emperor & the telephone
of Franz Josef. A stark Soviet-era switchboard with the buttons
of an accordion, all of its connections laid out neatly in rows

of black & white. Cranks & fiber optics. The ornate horn mouthpiece
of an operator from 1892. At the Telephone Museum this morning,
I am the only visitor. A quiet Sunday late in the summer season.

Yet, the matron, as ancient as the equipment, guides me dutifully
through the displays, throwing a switch to call up an illuminated hologram
of a statue—where is the original?—honoring long distance.

When she sends power into the frayed, paper-coated cables
of the city's original exchange, the massive matrix begins to hum & click
& whir. And a long minute later—delight!—the rotary phone

beside me rings. For Benjamin, the technology is heroic.
For it has prevailed, he says, like those unfortunate infants of myth,
who, cast out into the shadowy wilderness of the back halls, surrounded

by bins of soiled linens & gas meters, emerge . . . *a consolation
for loneliness . . . the light of a last hope.* The home's benevolent king.
In a novel by George Konrád, a man attempts to explain to his daughter

why he has had so many lovers: when the clothes come off, he tells her,
everything is discovered. And, he goes on, it is, in the end, discovery
we want. Though wouldn't even the most inventive among us find—

after so much disrobing—simply more of what we already know?
Shall I celebrate the counterpoint? The nearly infinite revelatory potential
of a bolt of heavy silk run through the fingers of the able seamstress

or the sensuous curves of the first desktop telephone—its molded
black handset recumbent in a pair of slender chrome arms. Meaning,
once I fell in love with a beautiful voice passing through the wire.

I remember the drop of it, a man talking about something he'd read,
turning to a page with an audible rustle & breath, whispering, *Listen.*
These are the lines that haunt. It's not that the skin has no function,

only that the tongue can play so many parts. At seventeen, I was haunted
by those protagonists who had no interiors. Someone asks the hero,
What do you really think of me? The hero's cold reply: *I don't.* In a month

the phone has sounded only once. On the other end, a pre-recorded message
playing in a language I'll never understand. Tomorrow, I think, will be
a good day to wash the floors, though no one will visit. Solitude: liberation

from even the expectation of being seen. Everything I do I know I do
for myself alone. Still, I'm thinking of you just now. Perhaps you'll call.
It's a silly, outdated sentiment. Where is the glass case to hold it? And,

beside it, what shall we write? Oh, something human, something grand.

THE CABINET

Memory is not an instrument for exploring the past but its theatre.
It is the medium of past experience, as the ground is the medium
in which dead cities lie interred.

—Walter Benjamin

St. Stephen's Eve, noon igniting Attila ut: the ochre-bright buildings
crumbling at their edges from the concussions of bombs. And everywhere

stylized names & symbols I cannot decipher sprayed in neon paint—
around marble cornerstones, across wooden double doors.

At the post office, a young man offers to walk me to the bus, which,
he is certain, will take me where I need to go—the depot in the next district

where a box of books I've been expecting is being held. I imagine him
steering me by my elbow, the way I saw a silver-haired woman

thread her blind mother through the crowd at the Hauptbahnhof in Berlin.
But he has, I insist, already done enough: stepping from his spot in line

to translate from Magyar everything the frustrated mail clerk has had to say.
Breeze off the Danube. Then, winding uphill, the resurrected weight

of my mother's legs propped up by mine, my arms around her waist,
as she tries to stand at the sink long past midnight washing her own hands.

We don't grow old suddenly, though it feels as though we do: *on and on,
from tree to tree*, the Hungarian poet tells us. A small boy is tracking

the stray horses as he has been told to do; farther & farther he goes
into the twilight until he finds the bread trail he's spread behind him

has been eaten & his *cross-twig marks overgrown. It's not a reel of film
or tape that can be put in fast reverse.* This morning I wake up

with a muddled mind; I type one word while intending to type another.
Benjamin held his ear to the 19th century & heard anthracite clatter

down the chute into the stove. And hoping to inoculate himself against
a homesickness he already felt, he called up each loved, absent thing

in order to better steel himself against the future memory of it:
his desk & an intricate toy mine with miniature wheelbarrows & lanterns,

the dark pool at the zoo where he had waited to glimpse the otter's
slick back. And the wardrobe from which he would extract again & again

the tidy packages of his socks. Rolled up & turned inside out, *every pair
had the appearance of a little pocket,* but the woolen bundles, once undone,

held no surprise. Thus, the mystery of the wrapping—also lost
in the undoing—became its own reward. This is how, he says, he learned

to read, learned that the meaning & the means are always one. Tomorrow,
The Sacred Right, the mummified hand of the Saint, will be raised up

in its small house of glass & lead & paraded around the square
in front of the basilica, grimly speaking as much for our cabinet of flesh

as it does for its vacated ethereal boarder. If each day here is slow
& predictable, no one who has passed through this other century

would call that a bad thing. All afternoon, stunt planes roar & spin
in cut-engine dives & dizzying formations above the city.

Fresh contrail loops scrawled into the blue even before the script
of the previous flyers has faded. Benjamin, tucked into his childhood

hiding places, became those places. *The child behind the doorway curtain
himself becomes something white that flutters, a ghost.* And if I vanish

into an old iron left out now merely for decoration on the kitchen counter
of a rented flat—oak handle smooth from use, a heavy rusted belly

that once held coal—what is there to be made of that? I lift it as I wait
for the water to boil. Outside, evening: purple, a bubble about to pop.

Below the window, a woman is speaking English, though my ears, unpracticed,
have to hurry to catch up. *I want to go. I want to go,* she says. *Where?*

Where do you want to go? A man asks. *I want to go,* she says, *to the river.*

No Lightsome Thing

No lightsome thing it is
To have been born a man
Now autumn closes!

—Issa

Mid-November, though some inner clock had me turn
a moment ago to February's calendar page.
Not the temperature, but perhaps the dreariness of the day,
more & more wind & rain. Still, just beyond the window,
an elegant bush continues to dangle hot-pink petals
despite the red mounting in its leaves & still farther on,
something climbing the mossy rocks gives up purple flowers
while whatever's advancing beside it brings forth blue.
This is the year my friend has devoted to documentary theater,
a play about Christians. When one character tells another
it's hard to live in the end time, the audience laughs.
I don't know enough to name the plants I'm seeing.
I can't say if they've bloomed here just the same
for a hundred or a thousand Novembers past.
The farm cat's stomach is distended. And that's likely
a bad sign, not pregnancy but something malignant,
lymph seeping into someplace it shouldn't be.
Perhaps some urgent action would make a difference,
but it hardly knows me & there's no one else around.

I can't imagine how I'd trap it in order to take it off
to be seen. When I open a book, I read that spiders
live through seven generations of the flies that sustain them.
One has woven a delicate web—you have to look very closely
to spot it at all—on the other side of the kitchen glass.
The onion-paper wings of a dozen ephemerae, long dead,
quiver there like tiny marionettes on strings. A daddy longlegs
hangs upside down in the damp corner behind the dresser.
Each morning I think I should trap it & release it somewhere
outside. But its stillness looks to me so much like bliss.
It goes on not doing what it's doing. This is how things are.

Angels Unawares

A stranger in the house of strangers:
                                       an enormous grasshopper—
carried in on a sheet from the line & nearly tucked into the cupboard

with the linens but for the muffled rubbing of its legs & wings.
Magisterial, as it was borne in an old pan back out into the garden,

there is no specimen to match it at the little museum on the hill
where I go later seeking the exact word for what I've held.
                                                    What there are

are stuffed herons & harriers, a shelf of the common Coleoptera, butterflies
& bees. A resin cast of a large sea-going sunfish, which here they call *luna*,

& a turtle's carapace, heart-shaped & golden in the places it has been waxed.
When asked to explain his inexplicable intuition for numbers,

the mathematician Ramanujan claimed the Goddess Namagiri came
& whispered formulae & proofs into his ear at night as he slept.

But because we are met here with wind all week,
                                       I dream now
only of home—all of the little houses beset by a gale so constant

no one speaks because no one can hear. So that when I wake,
the early sounds seem important, as if they had been chosen,

emissaries

plucked from the roar & loaded onto the ark of earthly noise, which is,
of course, all too soon creaking with the weight of what has not been drowned.

First, the urgency of the rooster, whose cry begins, after all, not in the dawn
but in the darkness & the propane truck clattering on its rounds.

A minute later, bells.
But because there is no music,
I imagine, for a moment, plainsong & symphony are gone, playing now

only in the skulls of those who could still read & recall them. Scores opened
at random in a relentless din & set out under glass beside a French horn

or a fiddle.
The staves taking on with time the odd, unanchored beauty
of equations. Outside, the electric yellow caps of cape sorrel & the white

of the mustard & wild narcissus are pressed flat along the headlands.
Daily another wire bearing power into town is unbuckled & shopkeepers

close their doors & wander to the cafés near the citadel to drink & wait
in the silence & candle-glow.
The old stories suggest the grasshopper,

like us, is thirsty for wisdom yet slow to be taught. Perhaps everything
it knows must come to it then in some other way.

Scholars at Cambridge,

presented with Ramanujan's theorems, concluded that they *must be true*
even though they could not understand them. *Because if they were not true,*

who *would have had the imagination to invent them?*
                                                    And perhaps
the grasshopper—twice again the length of one of the clothespins

it might otherwise have been—belongs to another world altogether,
a being delivered by accident on a ship of cotton bolls from the Levant.

And perhaps, blinded by its animal loneliness, it thought it recognized
in a simple wooden peg something it knew.
                                        The basilica in Xewkija

was built to seat two thousand; science, however, has only these few
small rooms.
                Its assembled host is unimpressive: a blue & red flag

flown to the moon & back & displayed with a note from Richard Nixon.
An antler of red coral. The shell of the urchin.
                                                And limestone bricks

from the old prison into which, centuries ago, the jailed etched their signs:
the imprecise outline of a hand, ships with oars, a field of crosses, dates,

but no names.
            The postulated meanings & order necessarily greater
than the sum of whatever is shown.
                                    In the dream, everything light

is being broken. My father's brother's wife, the one we called *Flower*,
leans into a battered hedge, the pockets of her apron heavy with rocks.

She holds one out, wrapped in what I somehow know is a letter,
though if I ever take it & learn what it is it has to say, I have

already forgotten. Just as whatever more there might be to say
about any of this, in the brightness of noon, is also already lost.

Perhaps, if we are ever visited at all, it is meant to be like this:
not an annunciation but a consolation, the page on which it is written

folded into a tiny packet & lashed with brown twine to a stone.

Letter from Cornwall

To Stephen Dunn

> How I have been helped
> By Jean and Madron's Albert
> Strick (He is a real man.)
> And good words like brambles,
> Bower, spiked, fox, anvil, teeling.
>
> —W. S. Graham

Here, the rain hammers even as the sun shines; in this way
it's not so different from the coast we know. Perhaps space,
despite the stone-built hedges, does not cut cleanly & everywhere
the sky shimmies sometimes just this same opalescent gray.
And if all the great logical-linguistic dichotomies turn out to be,
like the clamorous echoes of the gull off the moors at Zenor,
one voice, caught between the cliffs, switching back upon itself—

well, you'd hardly be surprised. And if some days the words
are less interested in the world than they are in their own making,
isn't it a selfishness we can forgive? The things get tired
of the ideas; the ideas, the things. I'm a little tired just now
of this body, but what can anyone do about that? Today
I understand for the first time that it is the Trengilly farmhouse
I see every morning resting on my shoulder. Washing my face,

I look into the mirror & out the window behind me
to this one visible human stitch in the scene—the back of a building
I've seen many times from other angles but have been so slow
to recognize from my own. Any big claim in all of that
is not about phenomenology or optics, but merely about
realizing, finally, how best to get back later to where I am.

Once you told me, *Every poem needs a Buick.* And it's true,
even the poems without roads, even the poems in which Buicks
have not yet been invented. Because isn't a Buick
just another way to utter the various desires: another bed
& wheelbarrow. The bower & brambles & the fox. The weight
& roll of the ordinary-fantastic, the empty-full. At least

this is what I am thinking as I walk the scrawny tree lines
gathering kindling between pastures of cows. I break,
as I go along, the broken limbs—some mossy & some as hard
& bare as bone—into even smaller bits & drop them,
without judgment, into the bag. What poem isn't a poem
about poems, even though we work against it? The cottage
has a stove & a night storage heater & sometimes—huddled
between them—I think *Whitman & Dickinson* & smile.

The farmer, a figure come alive in *Malcolm Mooney's Land,*
knee-deep in turnip rows & brown-black muck, sings
in the glooming the refrain of what I know now to be
his favorite song: Peggy Lee, *Is That All There Is?*
Beyond the last field, at Scott's Quay—a derelict jumble
of granite pilings—mussels glisten in a last shot of light.
One moment, marcasite hairpins there for the taking
in the seaweed's tangle. The next, so many dark object lessons
in self-possession, beings simply being what they are.

My friend is the local arborist whose job it is to operate
a gas chainsaw with great delicacy in the high branches
of dangerous trees. *This isn't a metaphor,* he likes to tease.
It's only as good or bad as any other wage. A barn owl
roosts in the abandoned biplane hangar, in a sailor's chest
someone nailed to the rafters decades ago with hope
that just this miracle might occur. This is the perfect place,
the perfect hour—everyone tells me—to glimpse its ghosting
off to hunt. I put down my sack to wait. Because we all want
to see it, don't we? Half for itself & half to be able to say
we have. Far from anywhere, there is no reason to be afraid,
but any stranger would be. The night ripens; a sliver of moon
appears. Happy birthday. How I have been helped by you
who track the shy & wild truths. The minutes here—
this, too, will not surprise you—do not pass more slowly.
Precise, the watch's jeweled escapement is, after all, nothing
like our own. It has no truck with the right-wrong heart.

Letter from Gozo

To Gerald Stern

Only last week, sick with a fever & retching, what I saw
were my mother's hands hooked to my wrists. One grasped
the rim of the yellow sink, shaking; the other held my hair
away from my face. I do not know why I think you
of all the poets will understand this: how my toes
sometimes seem to be my father's toes & the past,
a cobbled organ I have entered, thin as air, & somehow become.

The summer she died, I slept on a folding cot
beside my mother's bed, & one morning I woke
in the early coolness to see her stretching her hands out
before her, studying their freckled backs & thick knuckles
as though they were two splendid, bony fish. The hand
was Vesalius's first anatomy lesson, yet I can barely
snap my fingers. I aspire to grace, may someone believe me,
though I have been so clumsy all of my life. Here,
where the west wind carries red dust from the Sahara so far
rain comes down the color of blood, I tell myself this story:
to flail is the oldest two-step. The cry, I say, in its varieties,
is a folk song & the stumble, especially when it spills the oil
or wine & cracks the jug, is a kind of gross sentimentality,
a reminder that we are not, thank the gods, the gods,
who have never needed anything, not even each other.

For us, always the matter, the meat as well as the meaning:
the giant tunny, that eight-hundred-pound mackerel
whose great gray body the seamen hunt in spawning season
the way they have for four thousand years. Because
the tunny will always flee in the direction of open water,
because it is so easy to drive it deeper & deeper
into a maze of nets. And when the *camera della morte*
is thick with the panicked, living flesh, a signal is given
& fresh-armed men are rowed from shore & the ropes
are raised & the *mattanza* begins. In one report, old men
from Messina gently cover the eyes of the gasping fish
before they strike them because the tunny struggles less
when blind. Tonight my computer will pluck from space

your poem in your voice, the one about those who face death
by wind & call it forgiveness. A bird I cannot see will honk
from the one green hill above the village, the one
no one can climb because the high iron gate was locked
so long ago & abandoned. And when I shut the light,
I will be dreaming before I realize I've fallen asleep
with my glasses on, something my mother did every night
all the decades I knew her, which explains how
she was able, just then, to see herself releasing her fine,
muscled fingers back into a stream of August sun.

At the oldest temple in the world, no one pours an offering
or brings two palms together in prayer. Only a dog,
someone's emaciated liver pointer, wanders in & out
of the five eroded apses, sniffing the stones. And though
he seems as sore-footed & awkward as memory,
he has been forgotten, as even I may soon forget him,
who give him a name & some bread & the local white cheese,
which is rubbed with pepper & made from the sea.

So near the first things, the open mouth of the last. Tell me,
is it like this with you? For my part, almost everything
behind I go on carrying, even the emptinesses,
which are sometimes large & heavy, but sometimes not.
At the harbor, as they do along the brown Delaware
& in the creeks of the lower Allegheny, where the stubborn
musky runs twelve months a year, fishermen cast their lines
from the edge. They wait on their low, painted stools
& sometimes still, seeing their rods bend & surely thinking
they have lured to the bait something quick & other-worldly,
they haul up the ancient slender-throated amphorae instead.

The Festival at Nikko

How did it go,
The Festival at Nikko?
O Cuckoo.

—Issa

Sometimes we are asked to prove who we are.
Just this morning at the library I had to open
my passport & ask a stranger to vouch for me
so that I could take home a book. If you live
long enough, you realize that you are not
the person you were. Here in this kitchen—
a kitchen I might in conversation call *mine*—
I own exactly one sharp knife & the wooden spoon
I use to stir the sauce. A greasy tin kettle, pulled
from the back of a cabinet, soaks in warm water.
The days are like no days I have ever known.
Would I like things to be better? Yes.
But what does it matter? Intent seems so small
a part. And will. I have come a long way
to stand before this window in a harsh light
above a tap of undrinkable water. I pass daily
through the town's old gardens to see the peacock
in its cage. In the cold, it turns its back
to the opening. It holds its magnificence close
to its sides. And whatever this resembles—
shyness or restraint, a greediness even—it is not.

Acknowledgments

I am very grateful to the editors of the following journals: *AGNI, American Poetry Review, Blackbird, The Georgia Review, Gulf Coast, The Kenyon Review, The Literary Review,* and *The New Yorker.*

I would like to express my deep thanks as well to the many people and institutions that have so generously supported my writing: the Lewis Center for the Arts at Princeton University, where I was a Hodder Fellow, the Trustees of the Amy Lowell Travelling Scholarship, the New Jersey State Council on the Arts, the Rona Jaffe Foundation, Virginia Commonwealth University, and my editors, Paul Muldoon and Hanne Winarsky, at Princeton University Press.

Finally, I offer my ongoing thanks to those who have so thoughtfully read and responded to these poems along the way: Anthony Carelli, Matt Donovan, Ciaran Berry, Colin Cheney, Barbara Daniels, Adam C. Day, Elinor Mattern, and Laura McCullough. I offer my love and gratitude to the friends and family who lift me up again and again in so many ways: Mark Doty and Paul Lisicky, Francis Kaklauskas and Elizabeth Olson, and Joan and Len Graber. And to Larry Graber, companion in travel and life, without whom none of this would be imaginable.

Notes

My reading of Augustine has benefited greatly from Garry Wills's recent translation and commentaries, and his insights into Augustine's texts are clearly at work in "*Tolle! Lege!*" and "The Third Day."

"*Dead Man*" is a response to Jim Jarmusch's film of the same name.

Florum Principi, or Prince of Flowers, is the title Carl Linnaeus (Carl von Linné) preferred. My description of his gardens at Hammarby is based on the information provided by Uppsala University (http://www.hammarby.uu.se/LHeng.html) and by Sally Hassan in her article "In the Garden of Linnaeus," which originally appeared in *The New York Times* on June 25, 1989. This poem also refers to Richard Preston's *New Yorker* essay "An Error in the Code" (August 13, 2007).

"The Drunkenness of Noah" and "The Heresies" owe much to Jean-Louis Chrétien's *Hand to Hand: Listening to the Work of Art*, translated by Stephen E. Lewis. "The Heresies" also refers to Ian Parker's essay "The Gift," which appeared in *The New Yorker* on August 2, 2004.

"*Fitzcarraldo*" is a response to Werner Herzog's film of the same name, and it is dedicated to Aaron Balkan.

"*Un Chien Andalou*" is a film (1929) by Luis Buñuel and Salvador Dalí.

The film under consideration in "The Synthetic A Priori" is *From Hell It Came*.

The inspiration for "The Eternal City" was Joseph Brodsky's essay "Homage to Marcus Aurelius." The epigraphs are from George Long's translation of *The Meditations*.

This cycle is dedicated to Anthony Carelli: the least imperial person I know, extraordinary reader and friend.

The passage quoted in "Another Poem about Trains" is from Milan Kundera's *The Curtain: An Essay in Seven Parts*.

"Three Poems for Walter Benjamin" and "Some Great Desire" respond to and incorporate sections of Benjamin's essay "Berlin Childhood around 1900." The translation is by Howard Eiland. My interest in the George Konrád was sparked by Michael Blumenthal's collection of essays *When History Enters the House*. And the moment in Konrád's novel that is alluded to in "The Telephone" is also one of the subjects of Blumenthal's considerations.

The description of the tunny slaughter in "To Gerald Stern" is based on the information provided in Ernle Bradford's *Mediterranean: Portrait of a Sea*.

The haiku of Kobayashi Issa have been taken from *Autumn Wind Haiku*. The translator is Lewis Mackenzie.